Printed in the United States of America
ISBN- 13 978-1537709505
ISBN-10: 153770950X

The Pretty Letter P Book
Original Letters

By Peggy Louise Parrish

A "You're Welcome to Color Book"

Dear Coloring Artist,

It is my desire to share my fanciful designs of letter P with you. You can make a few in house copies for yourself to try different colors and techniques. You can print them up as a card for a loved one if you want. The rights to the design are mine. The coloring is all up to you. Prisma colored pencils and small tip sharpie pens are my favorite. You can use any medium you like. If you print your favorite colored letter onto card stock you may even want to add embellishments. Hopefully you will be triggered to sketch and color some of your own. From one artist to another I encourage you to unwind your busy thoughts by COLORING. "Things go better with color"! No one will tell you how to color these letters. Some are shown to you in color to give suggestions. Ultimately it's up to the artist within you.

If you like this book, just wait and see the others soon to come.

* Please remember to place a piece of scrap paper under any work you are doing with markers

ENJOY

Creator of this book

Peggy Parrish

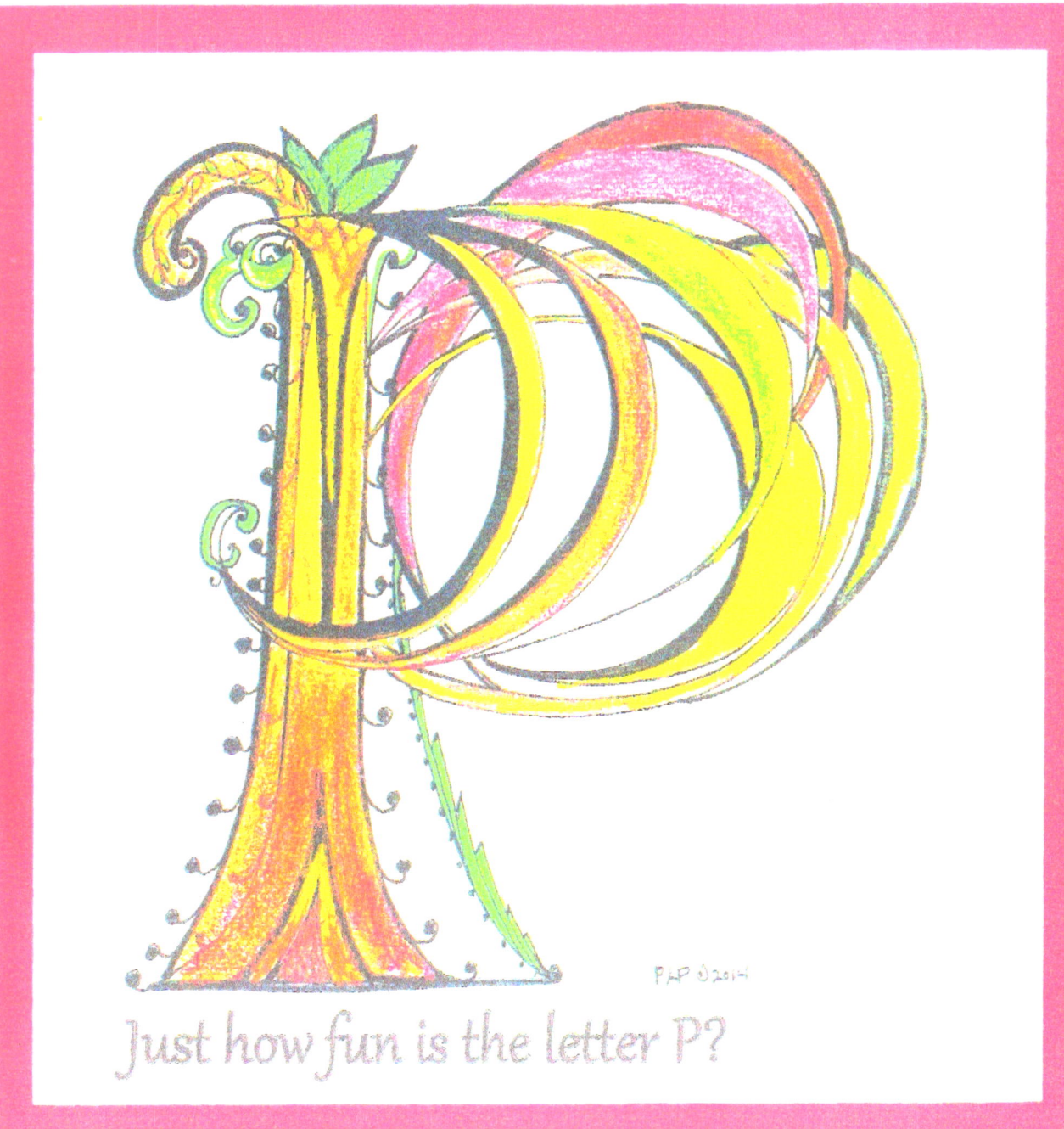

Just how fun is the letter P?

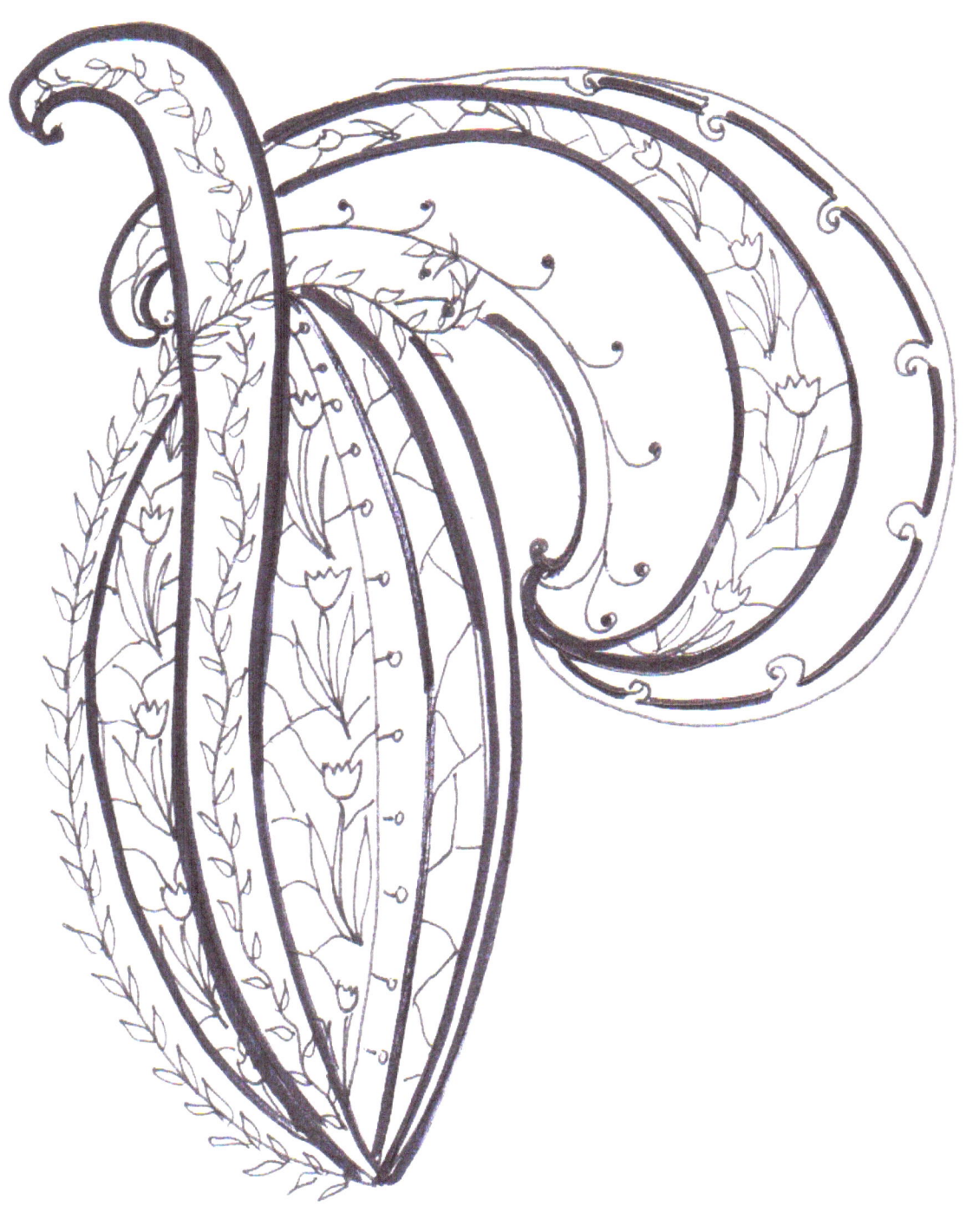

PLP c.2014

PLP c.

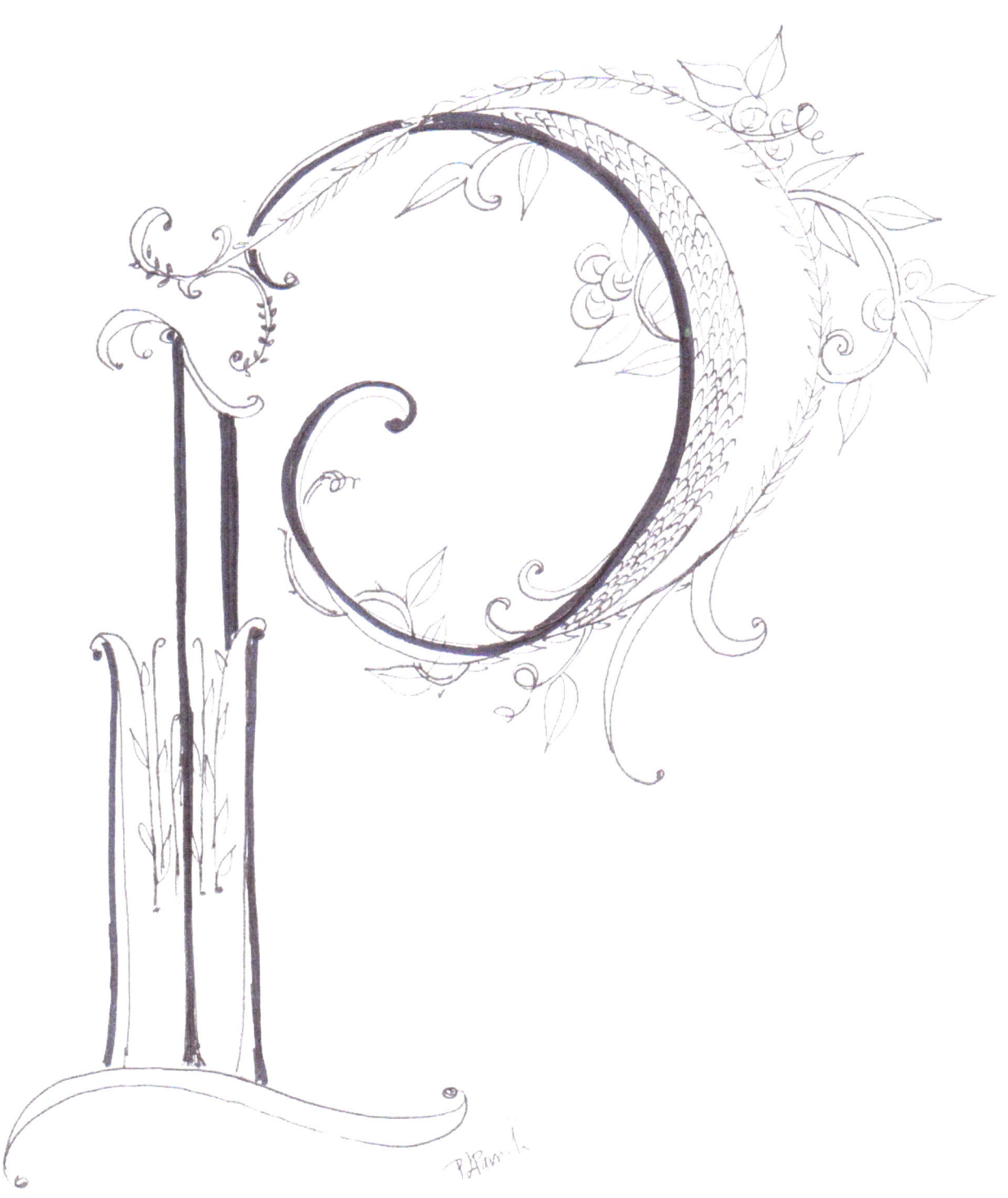

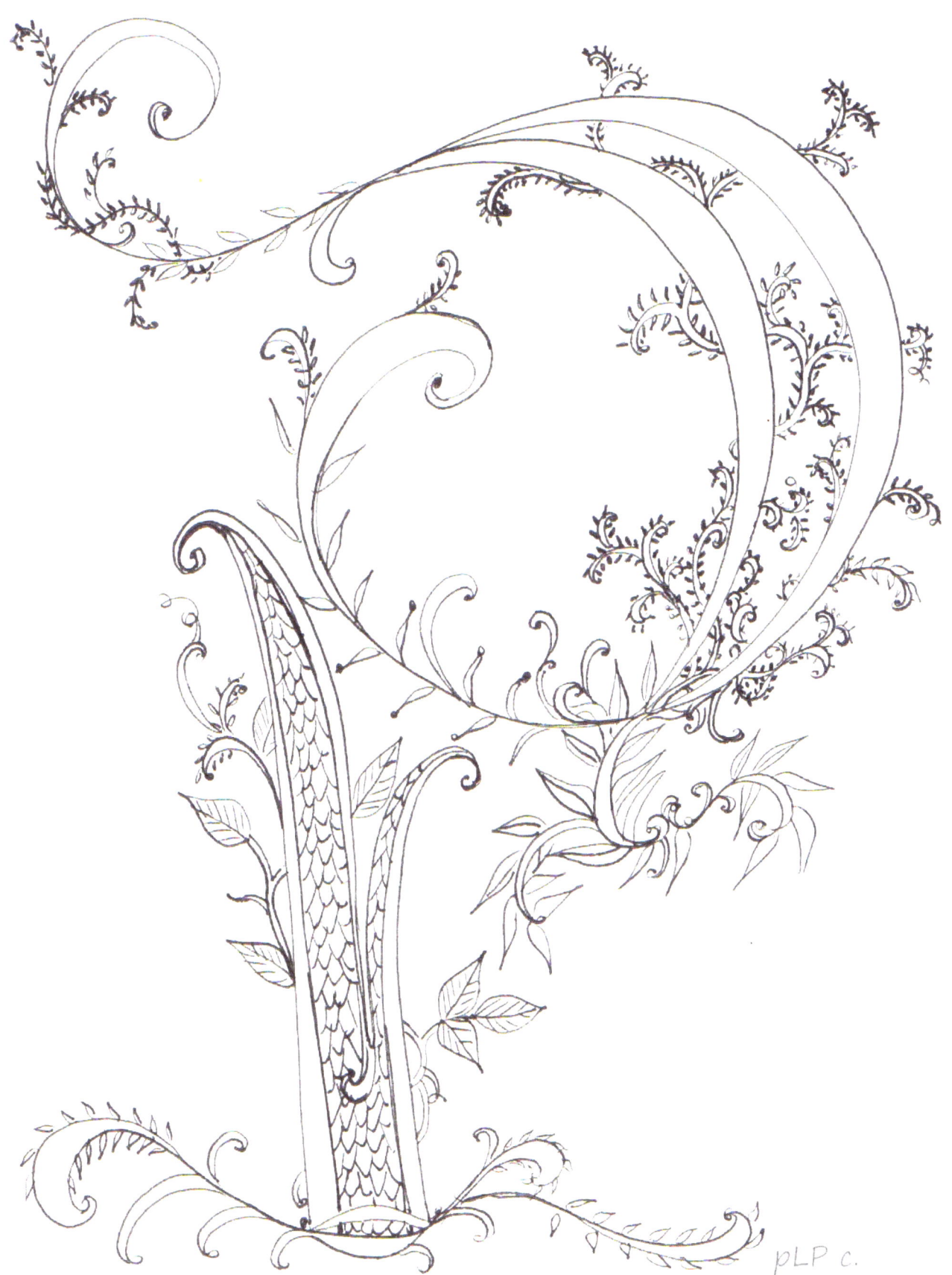

PLP c.

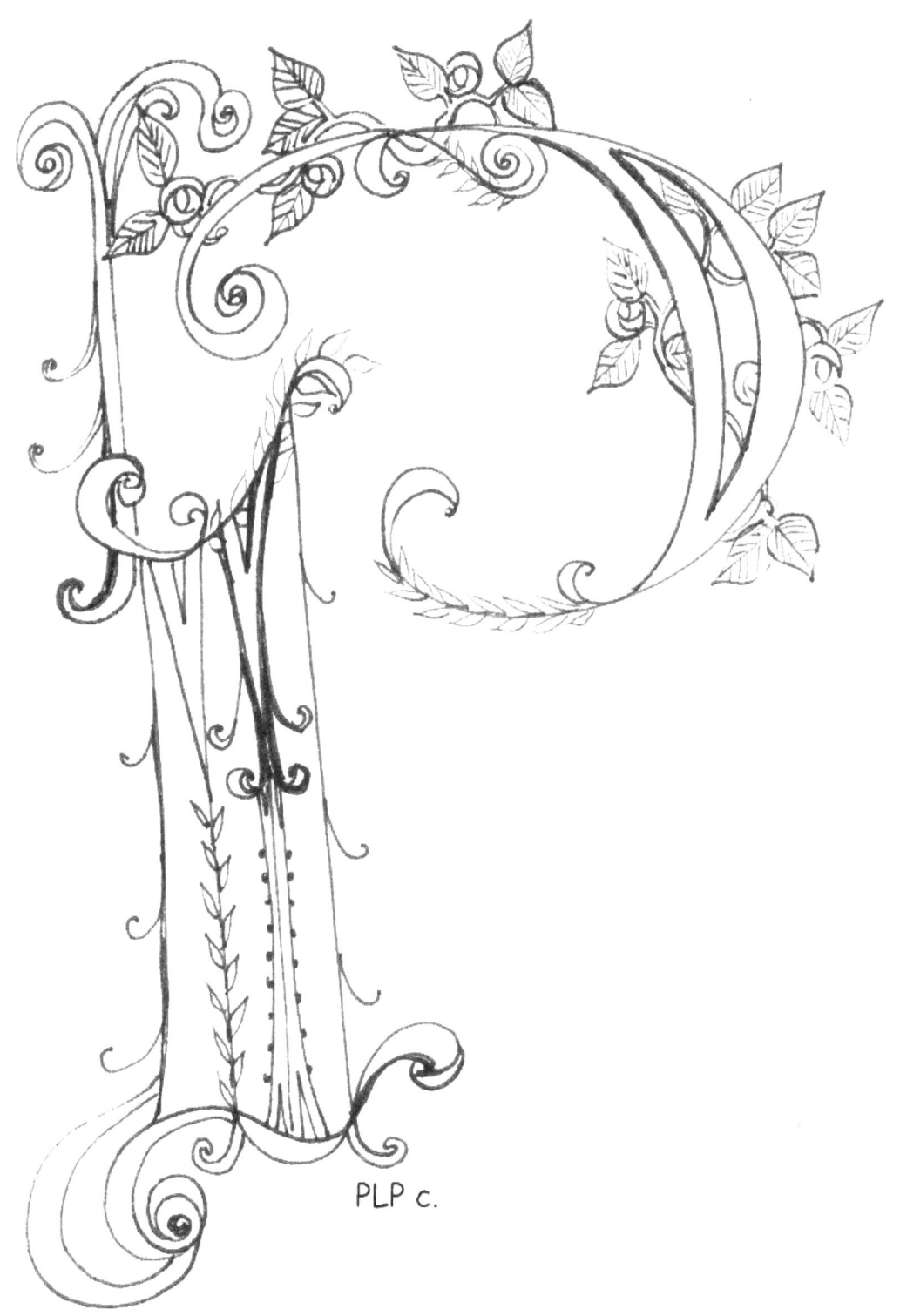

PLP c.

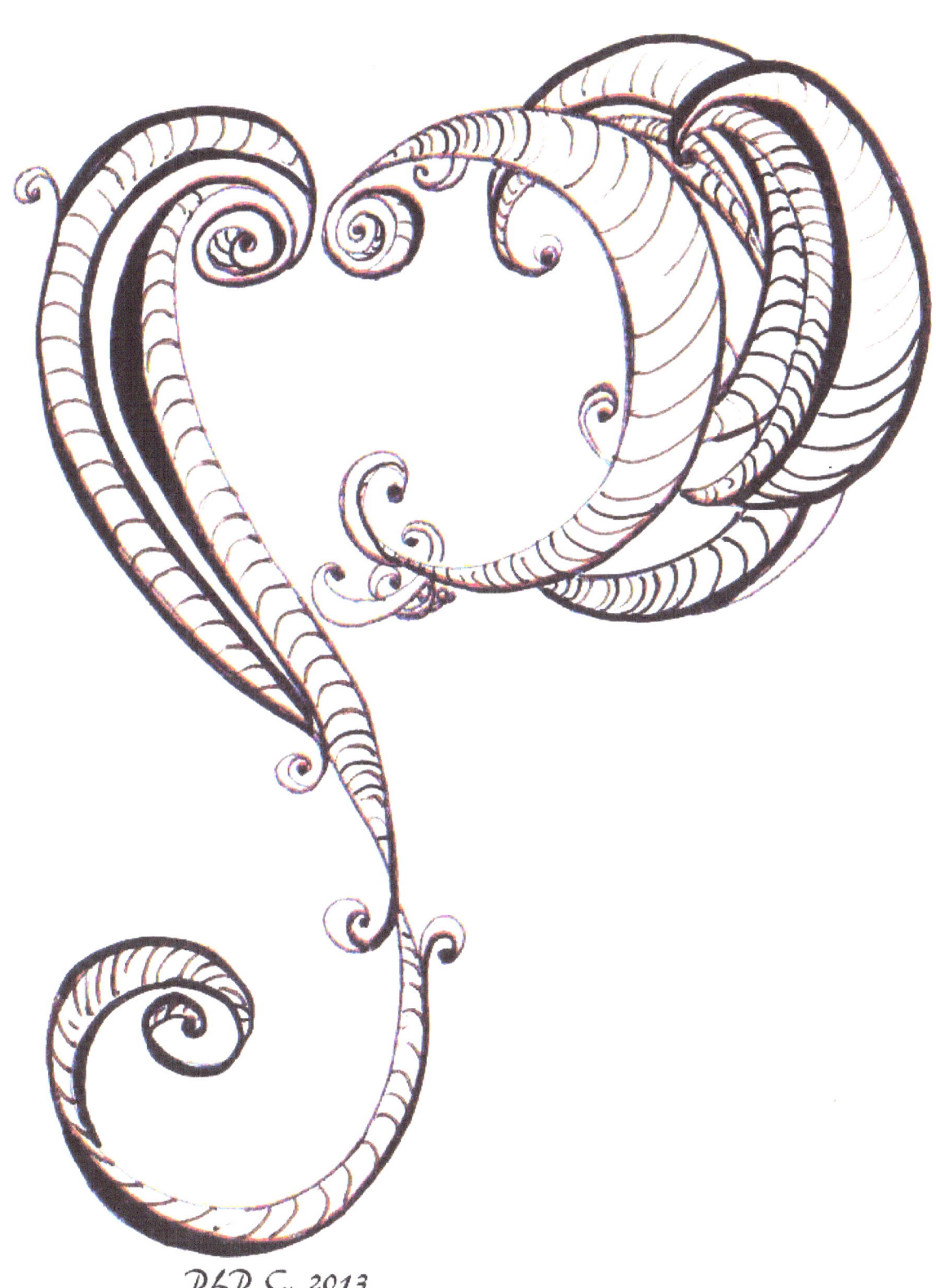

PLP C. 2013

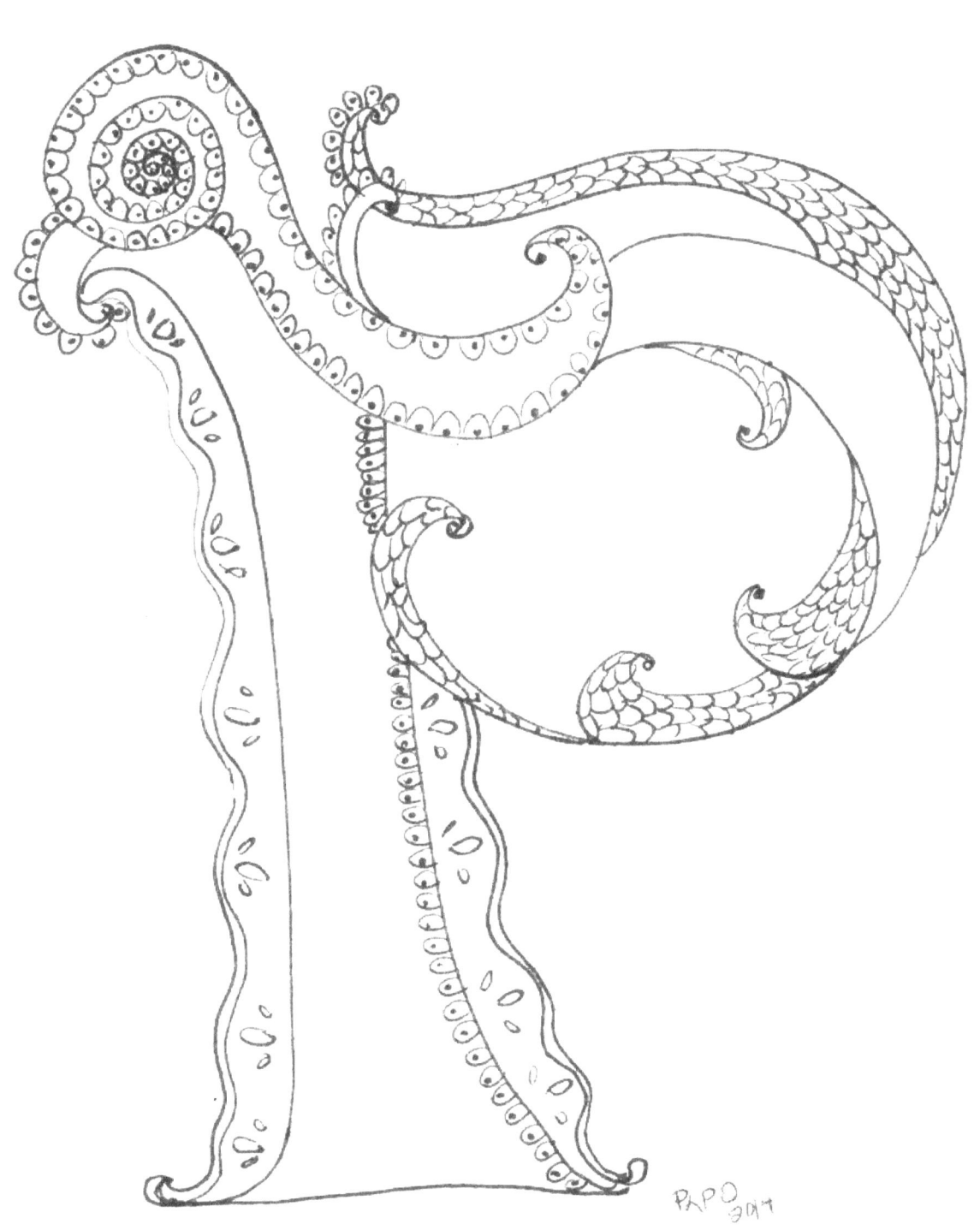

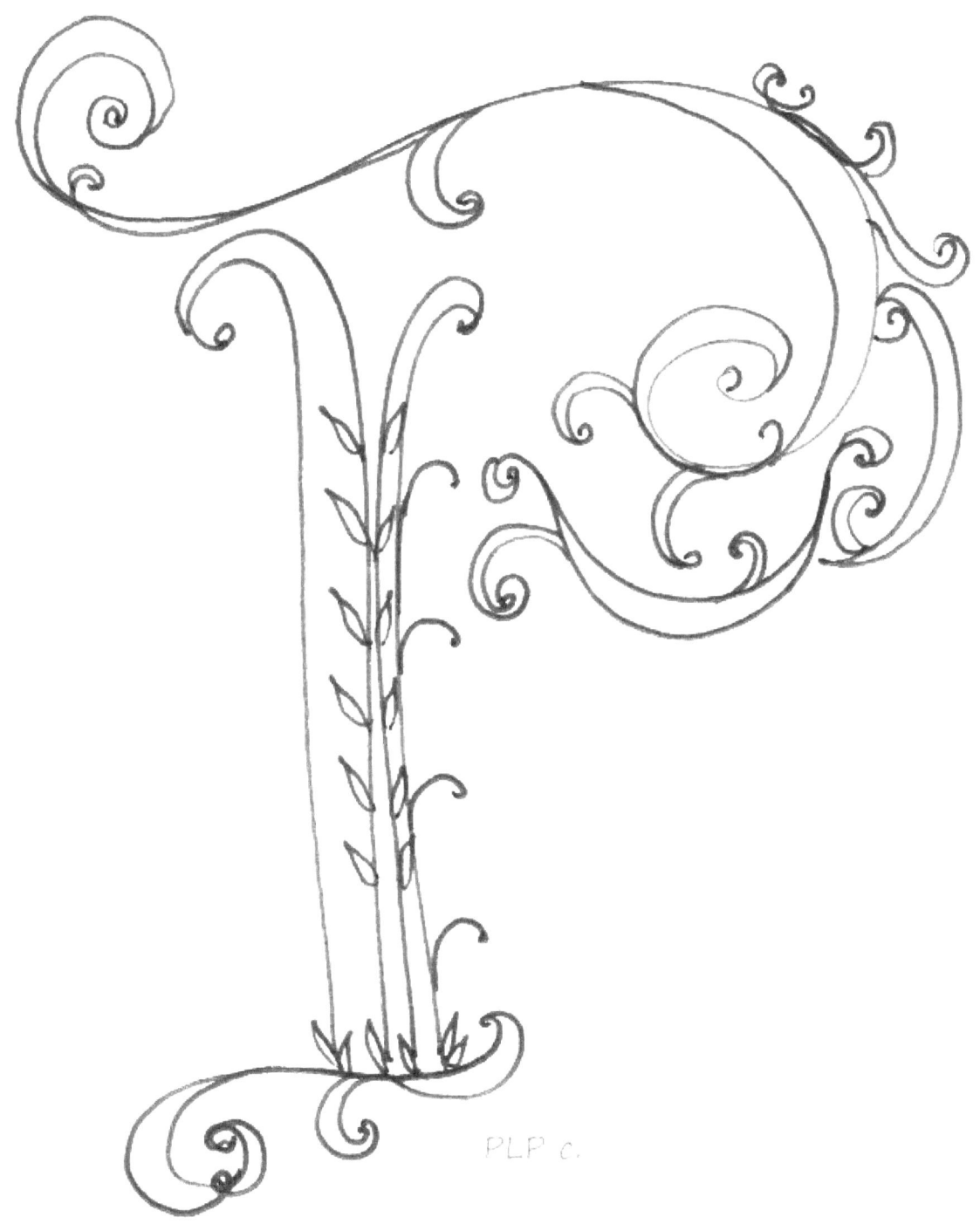

PLP c.

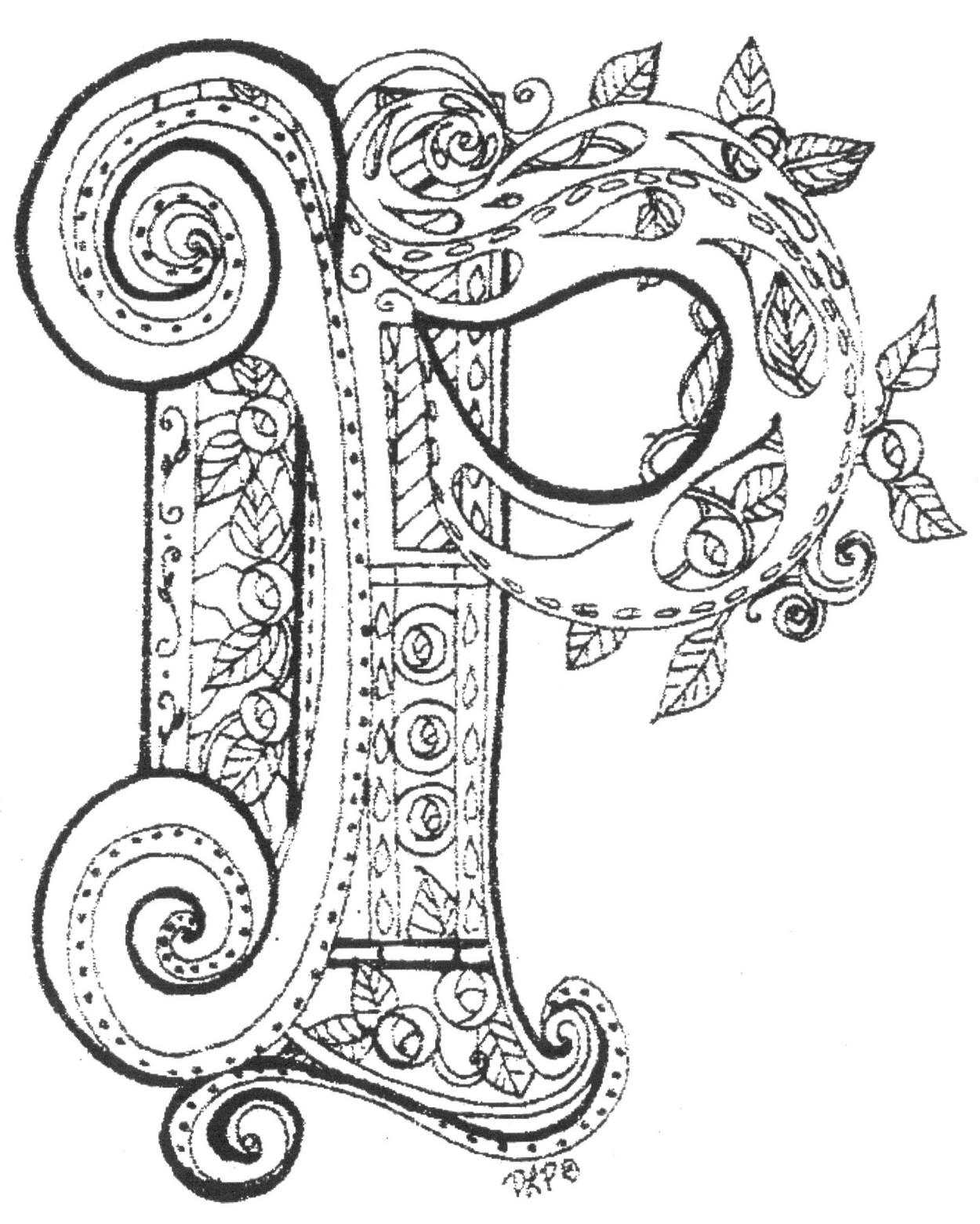

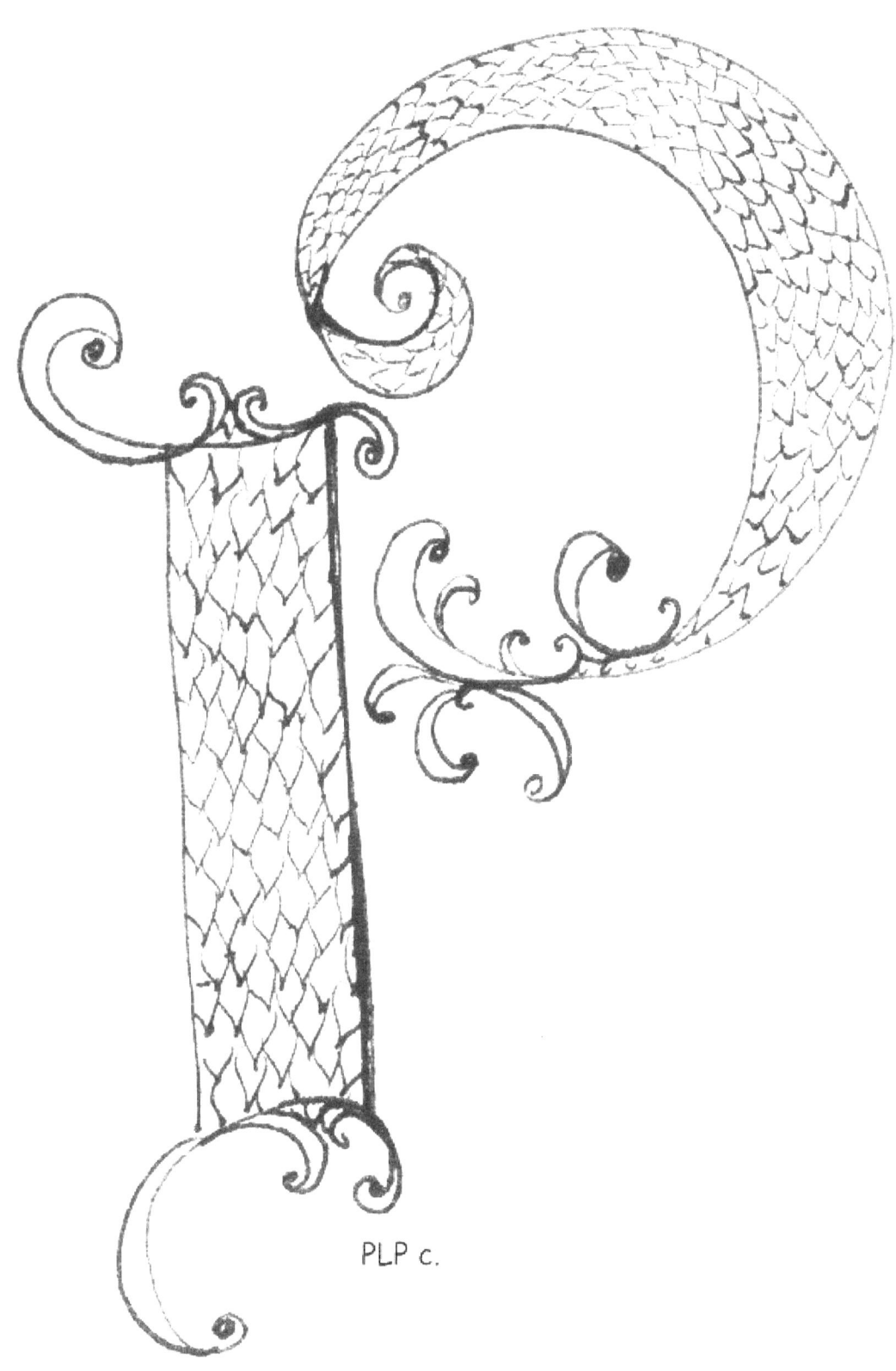

PLP c.

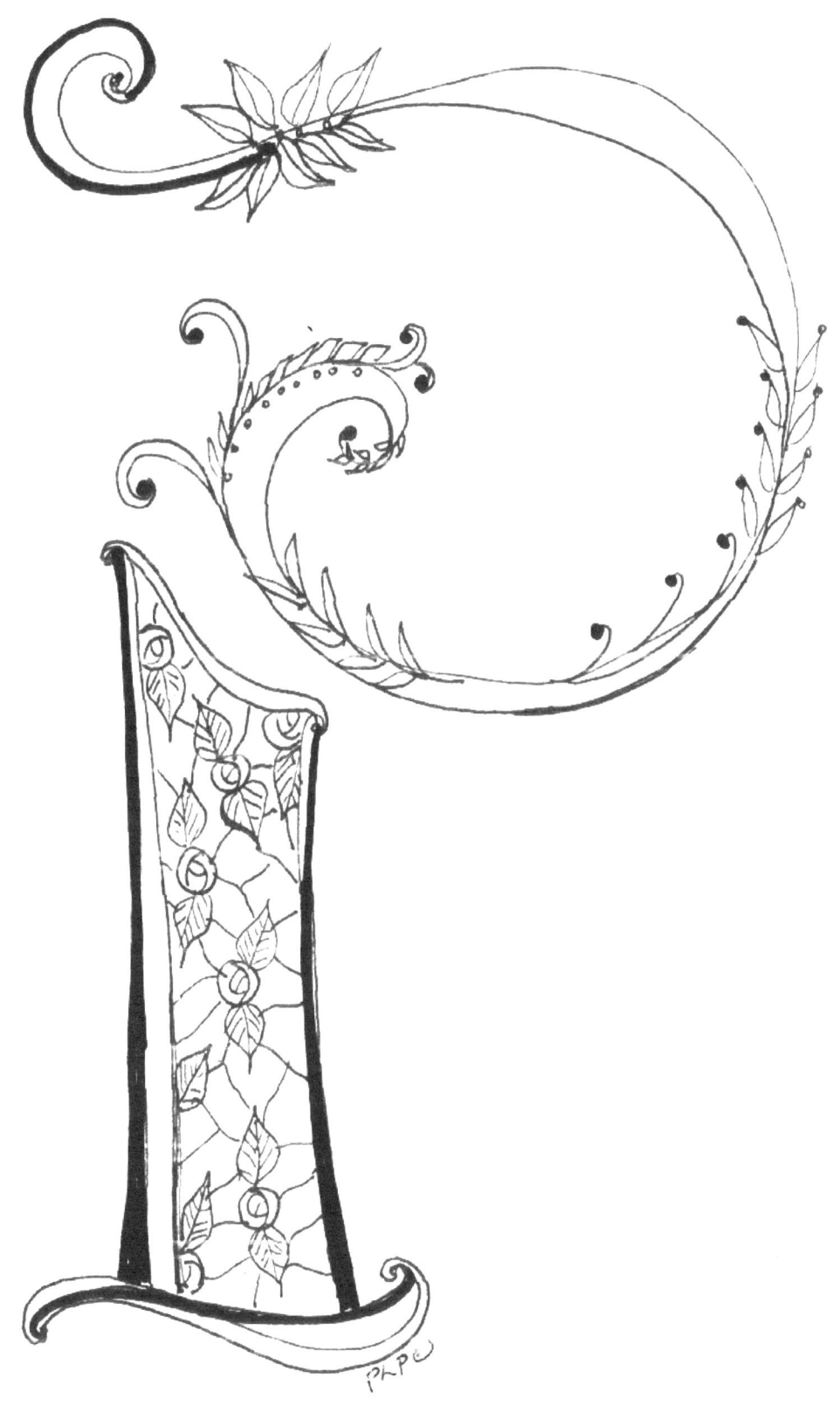

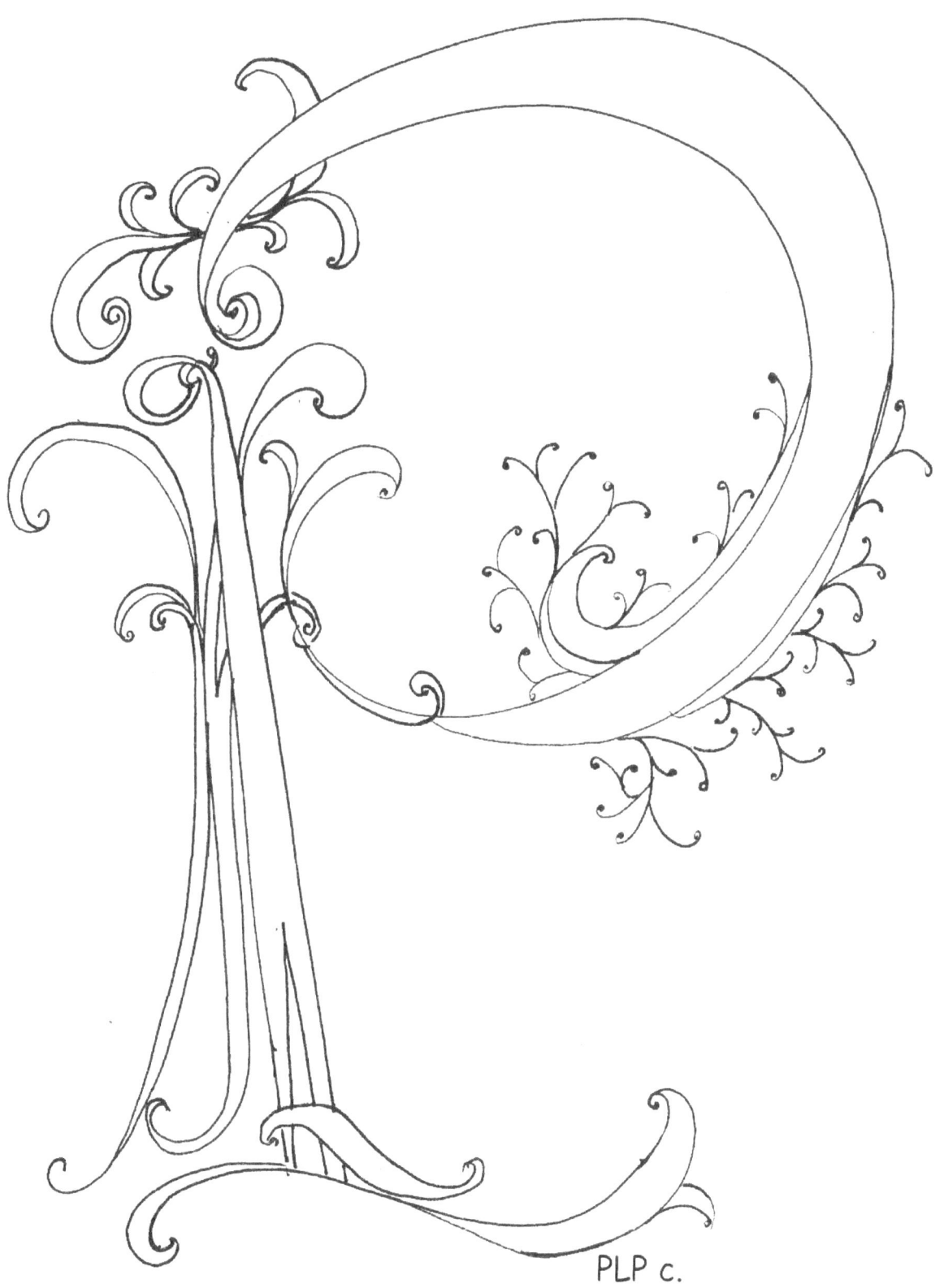

PLP c.

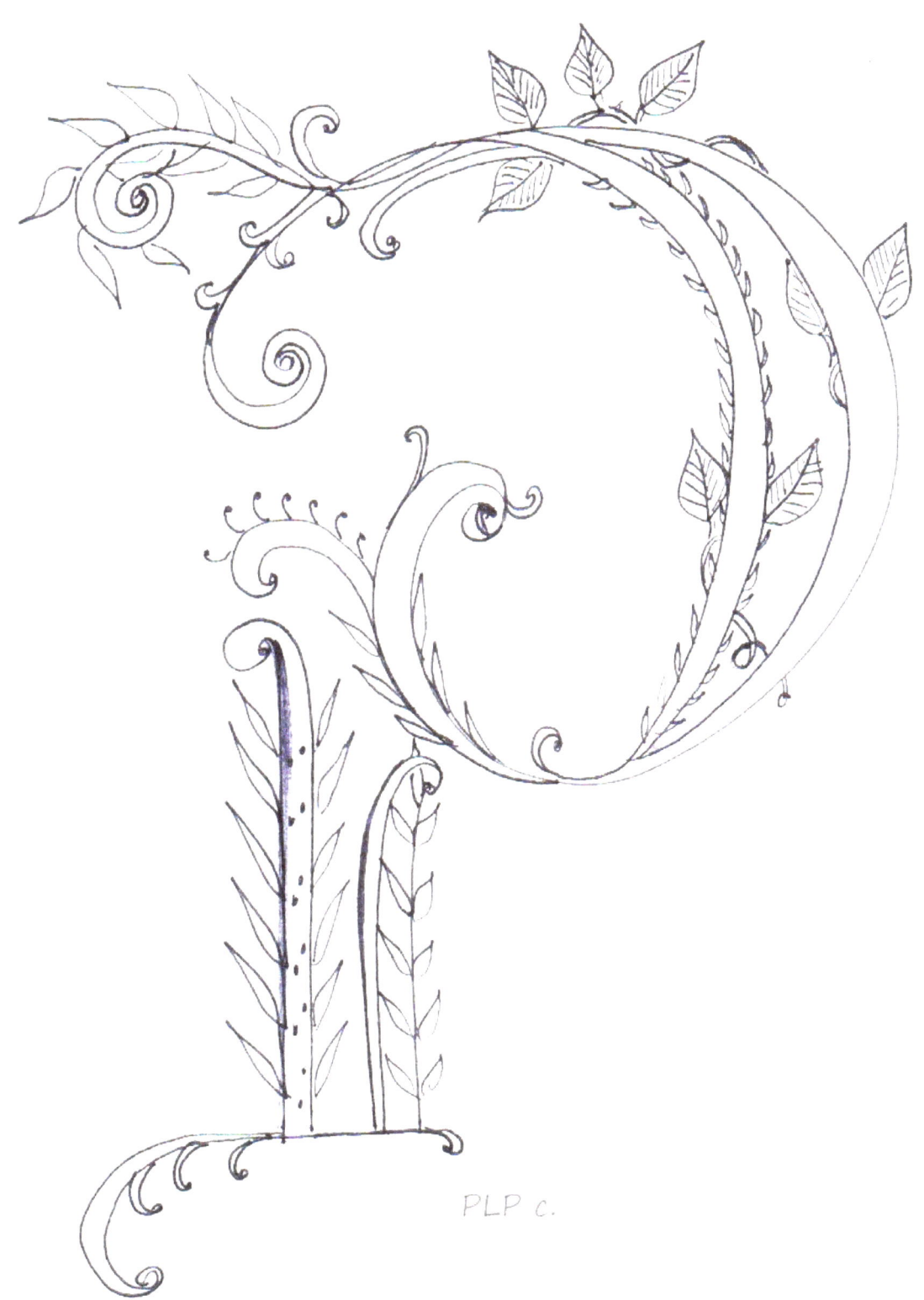

PLP c.

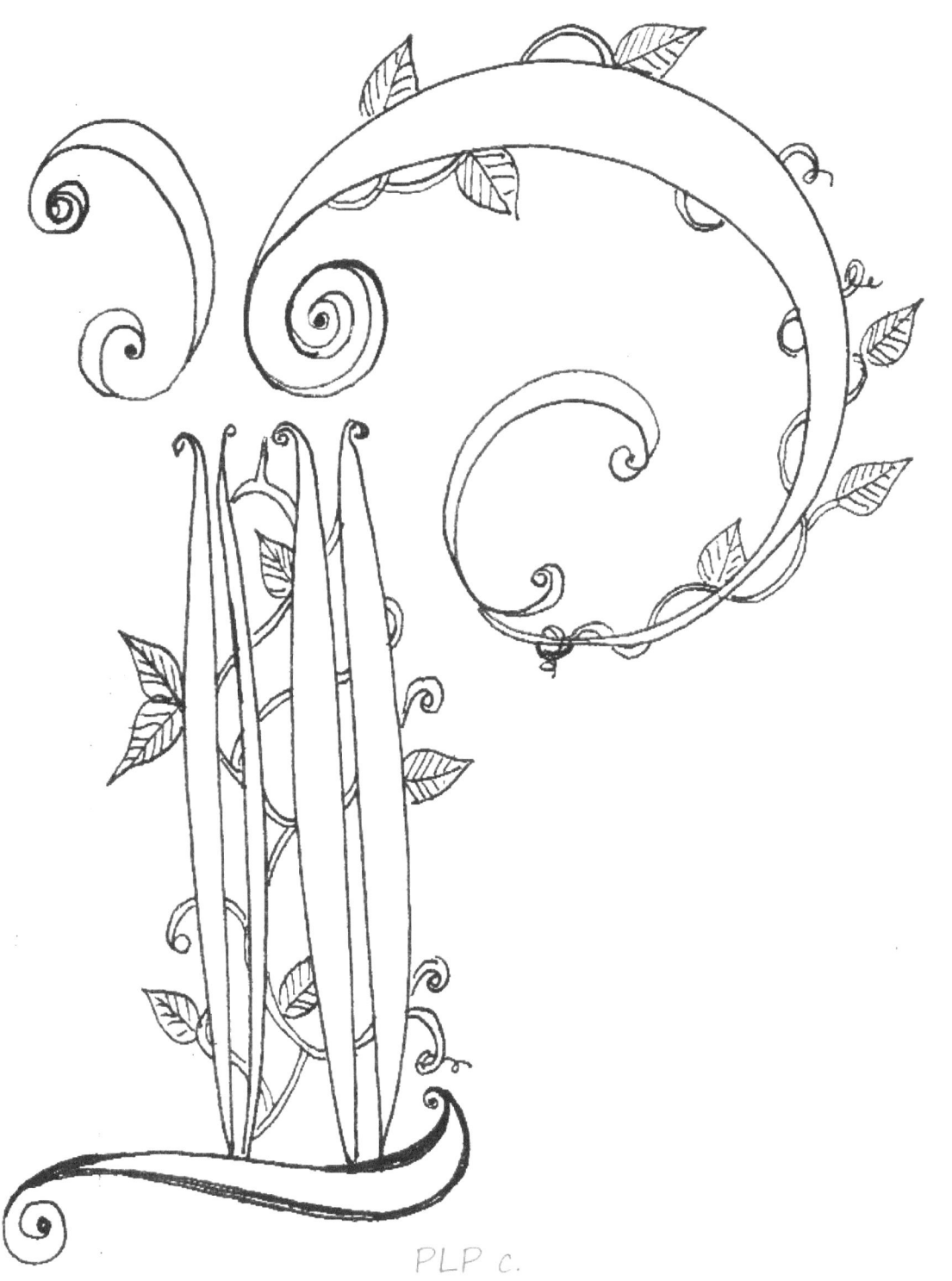

PLP c.

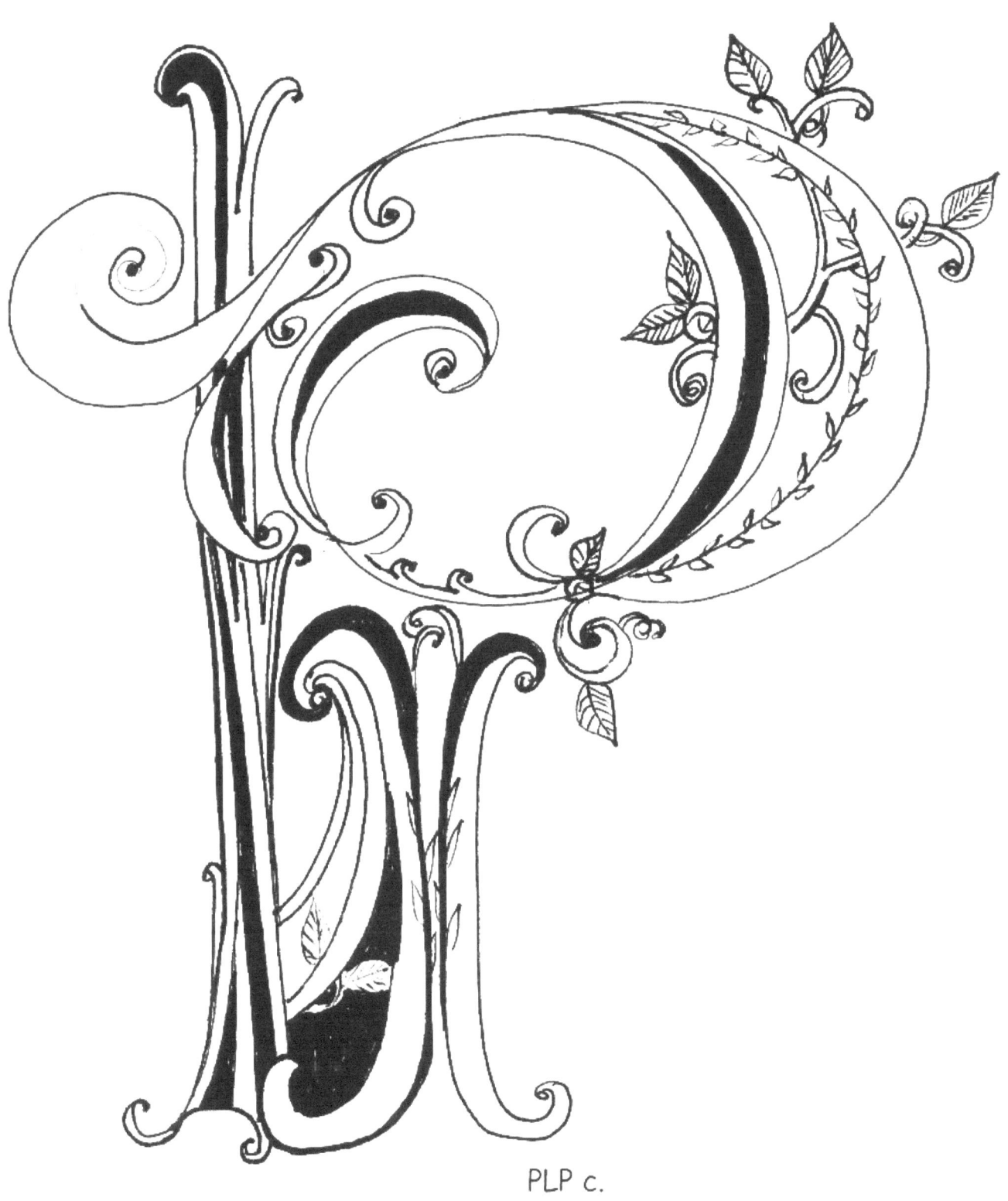

PLP c.

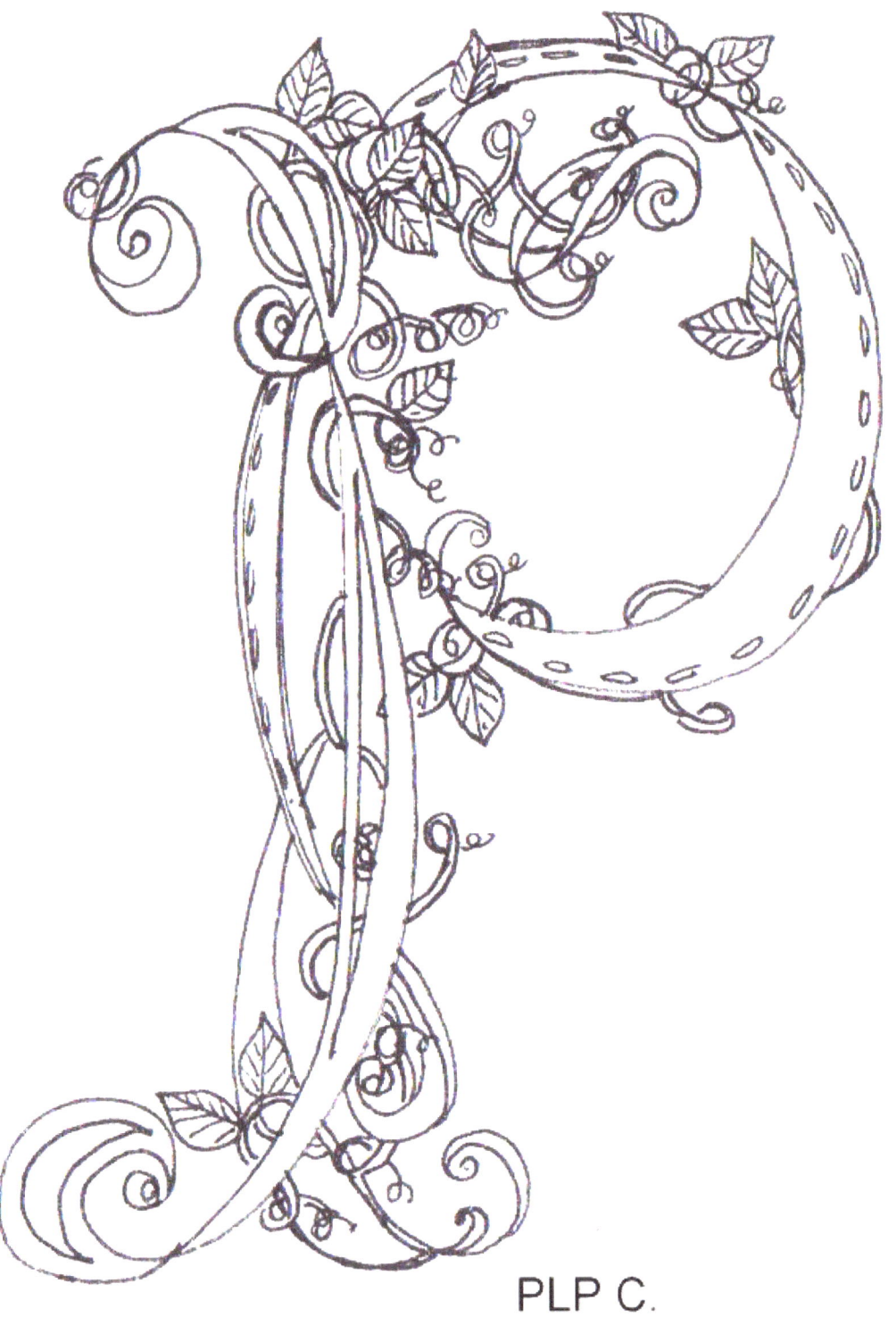

PLP C.

D&P 2010

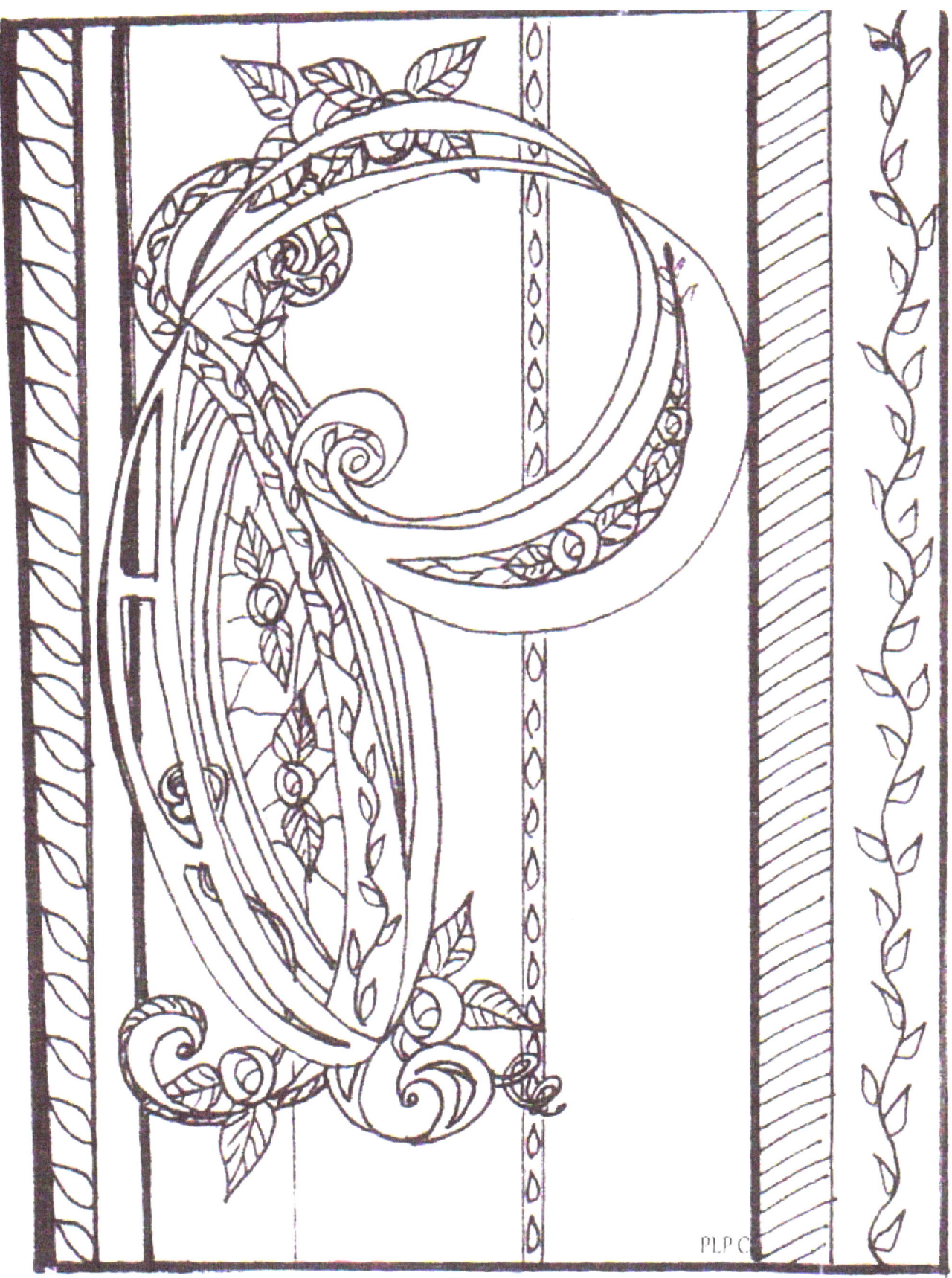

PLP C

43

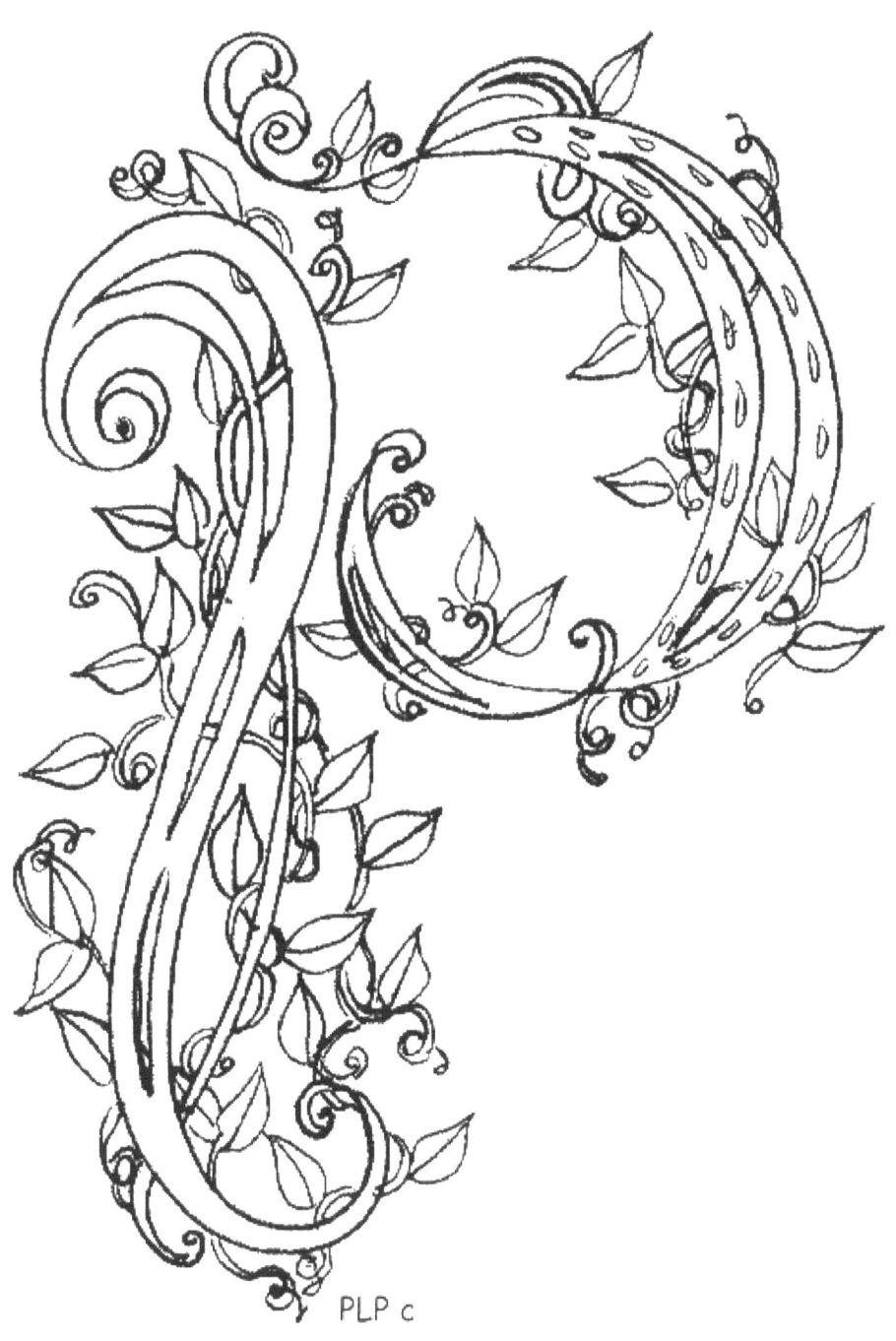

PLP c

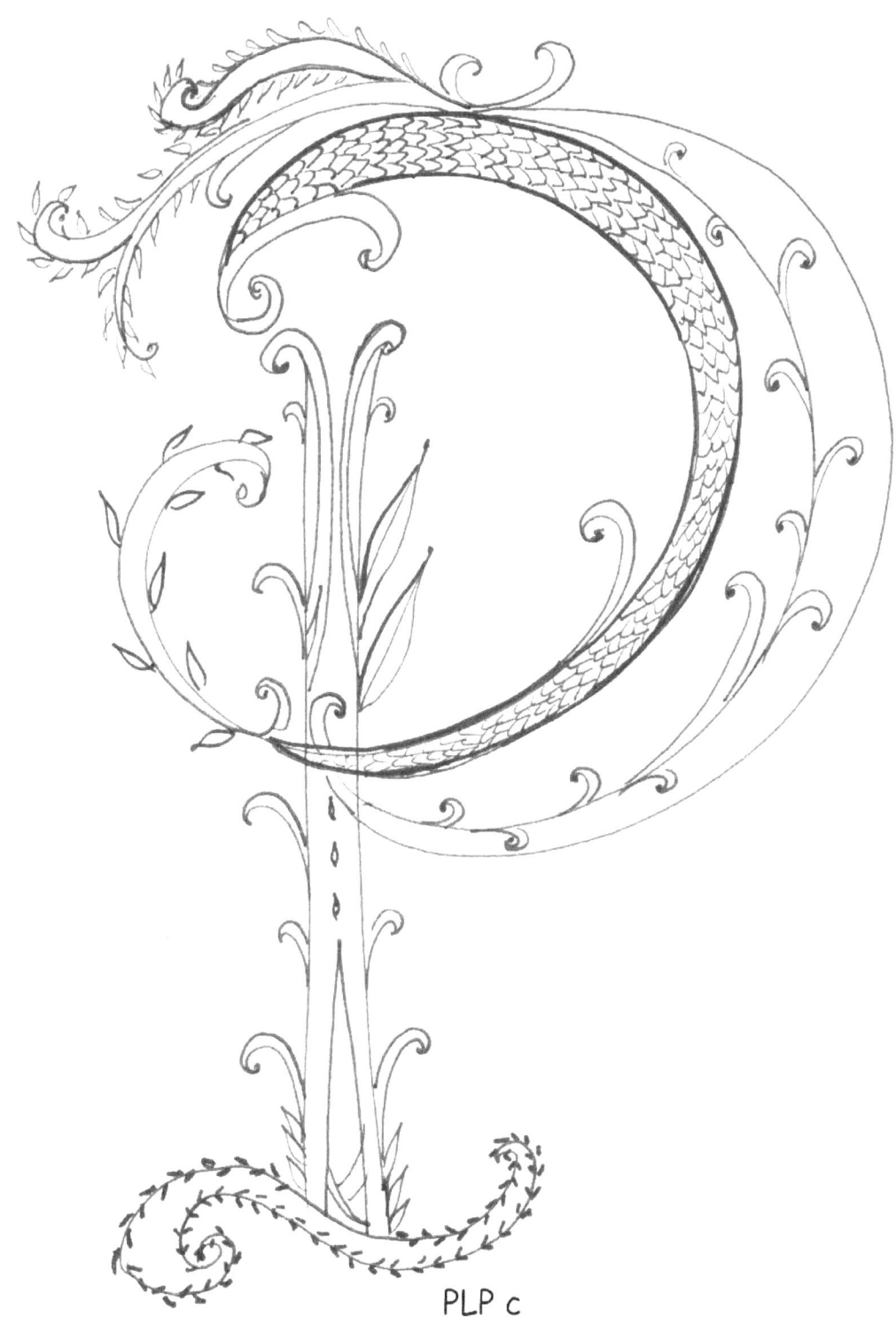

PLP c

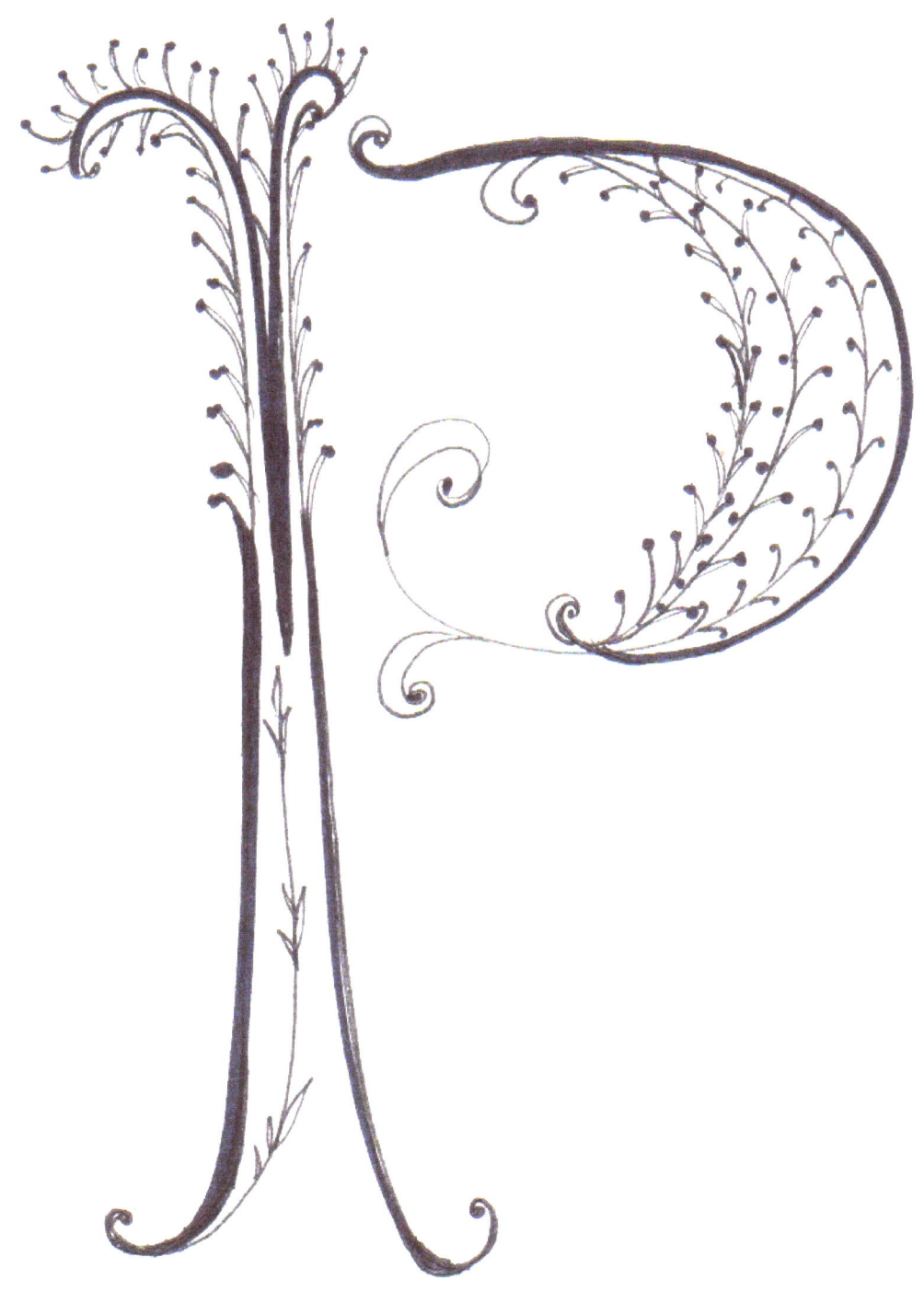

PLP c.

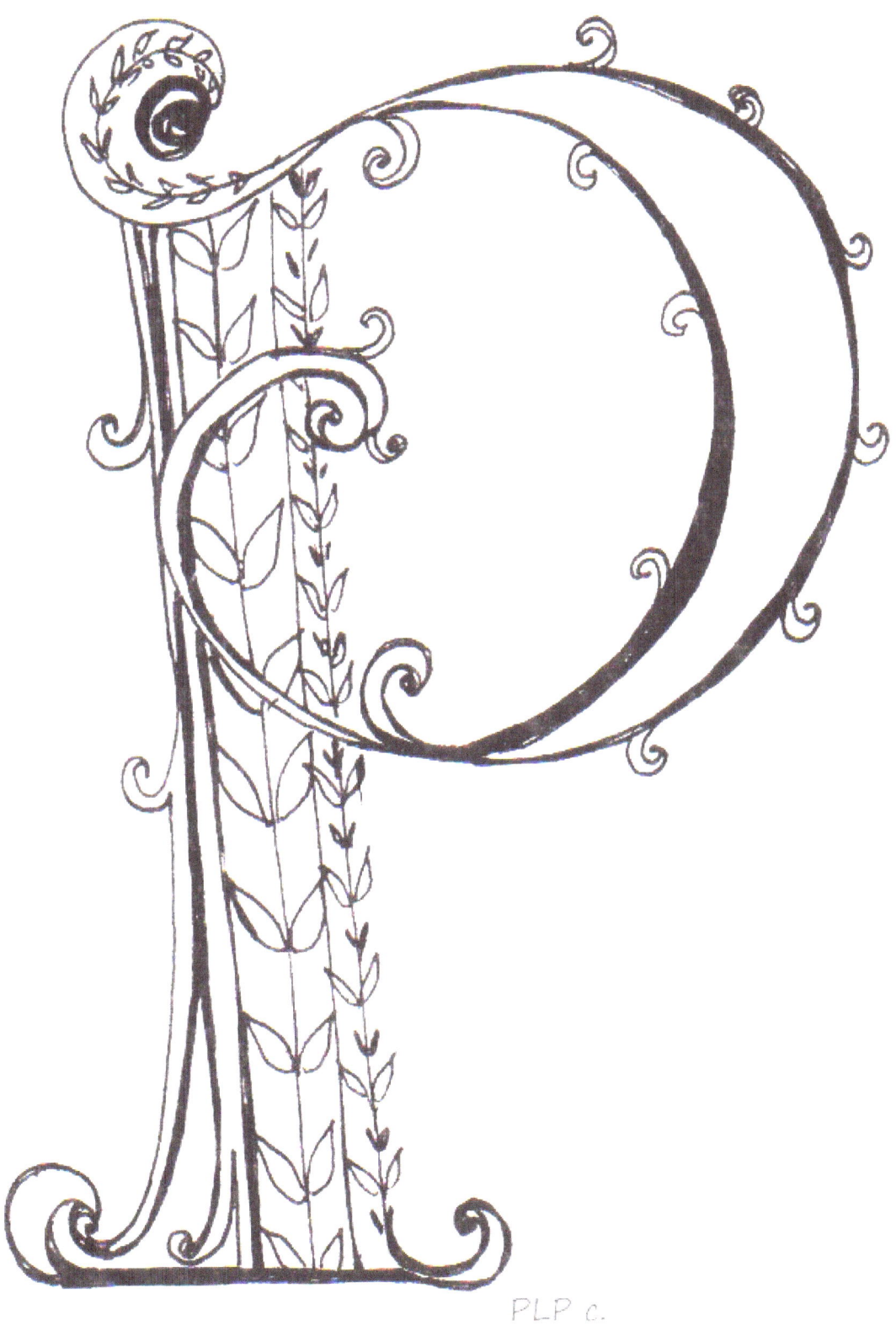

PLP c.

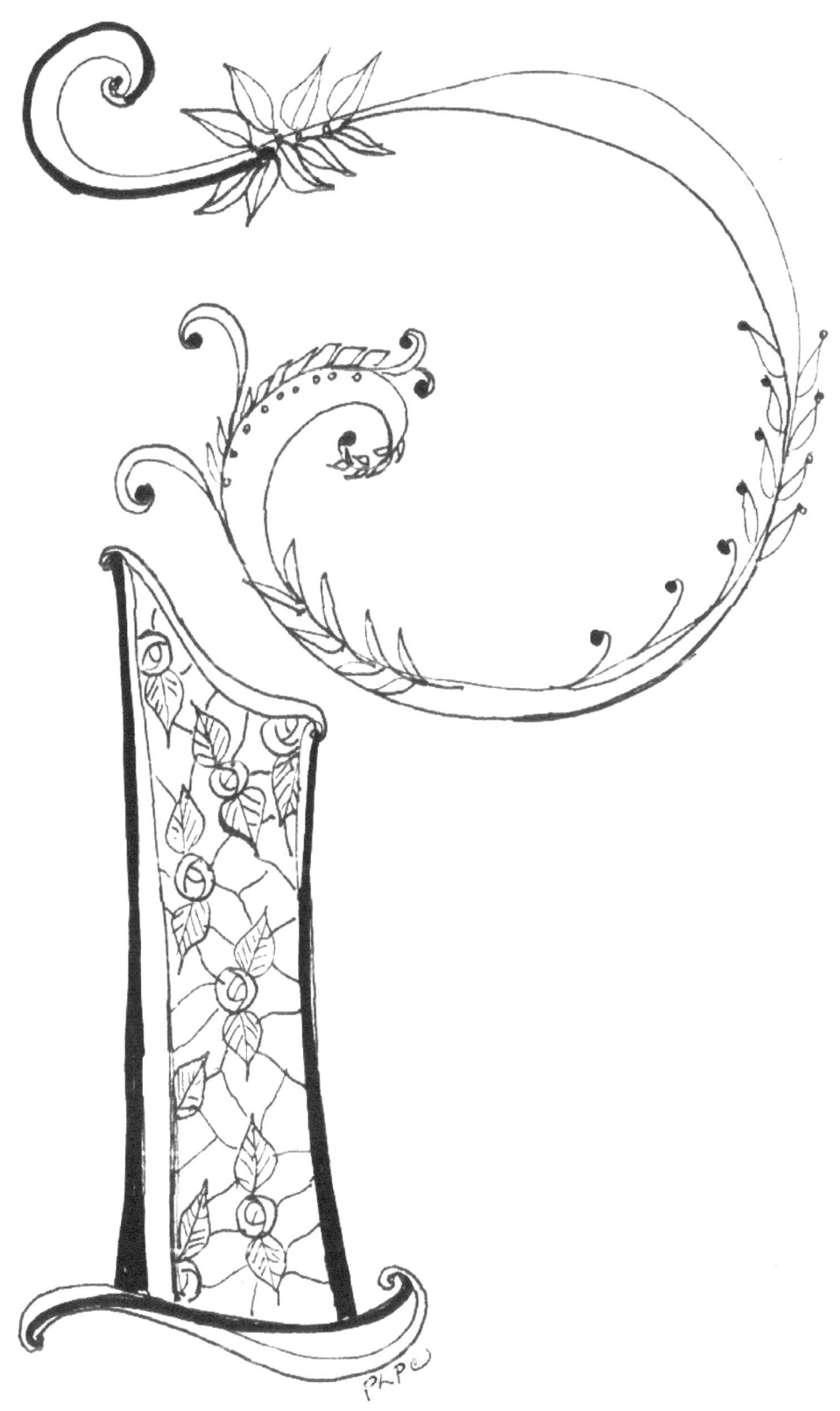

53

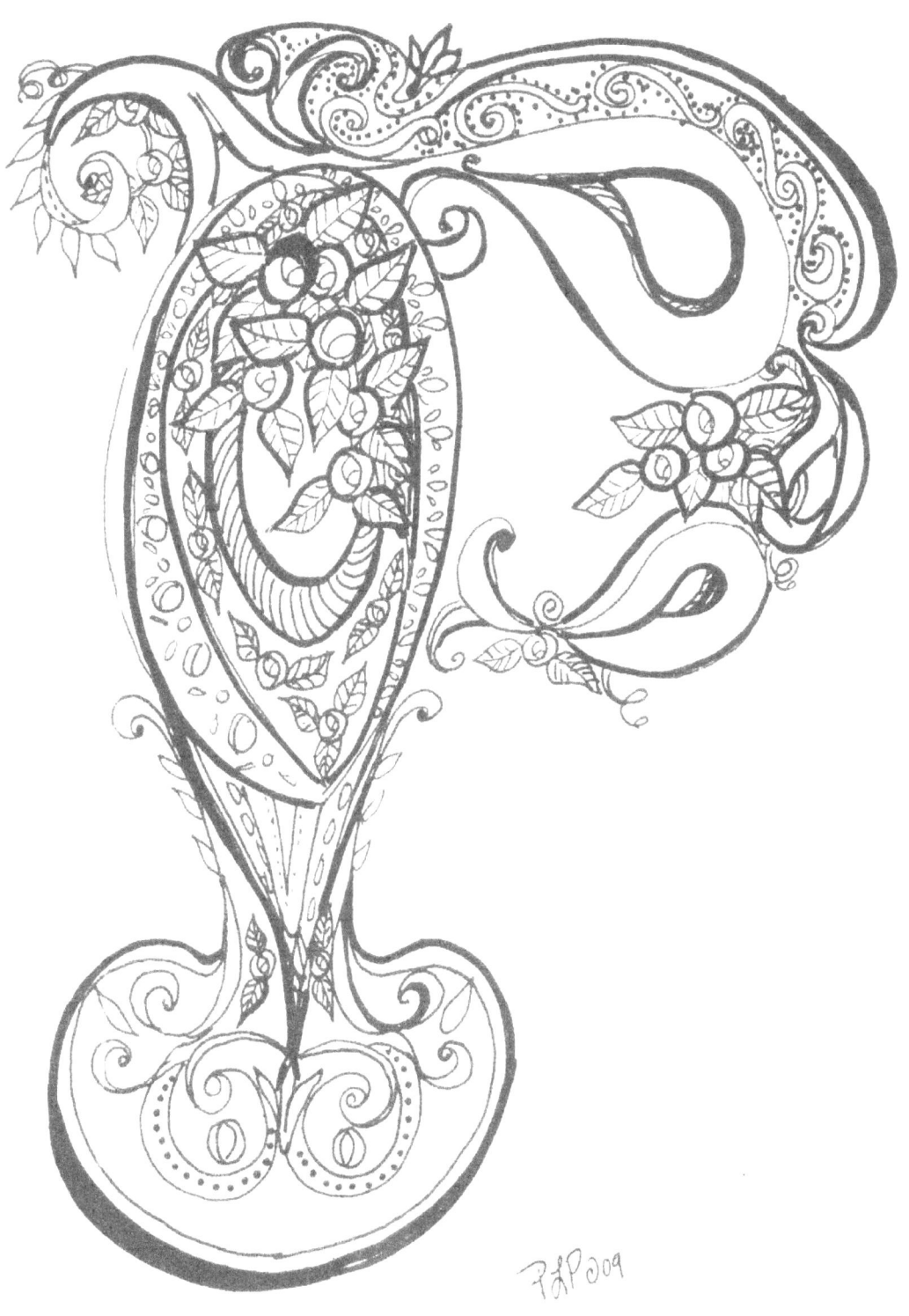

PdP 2009

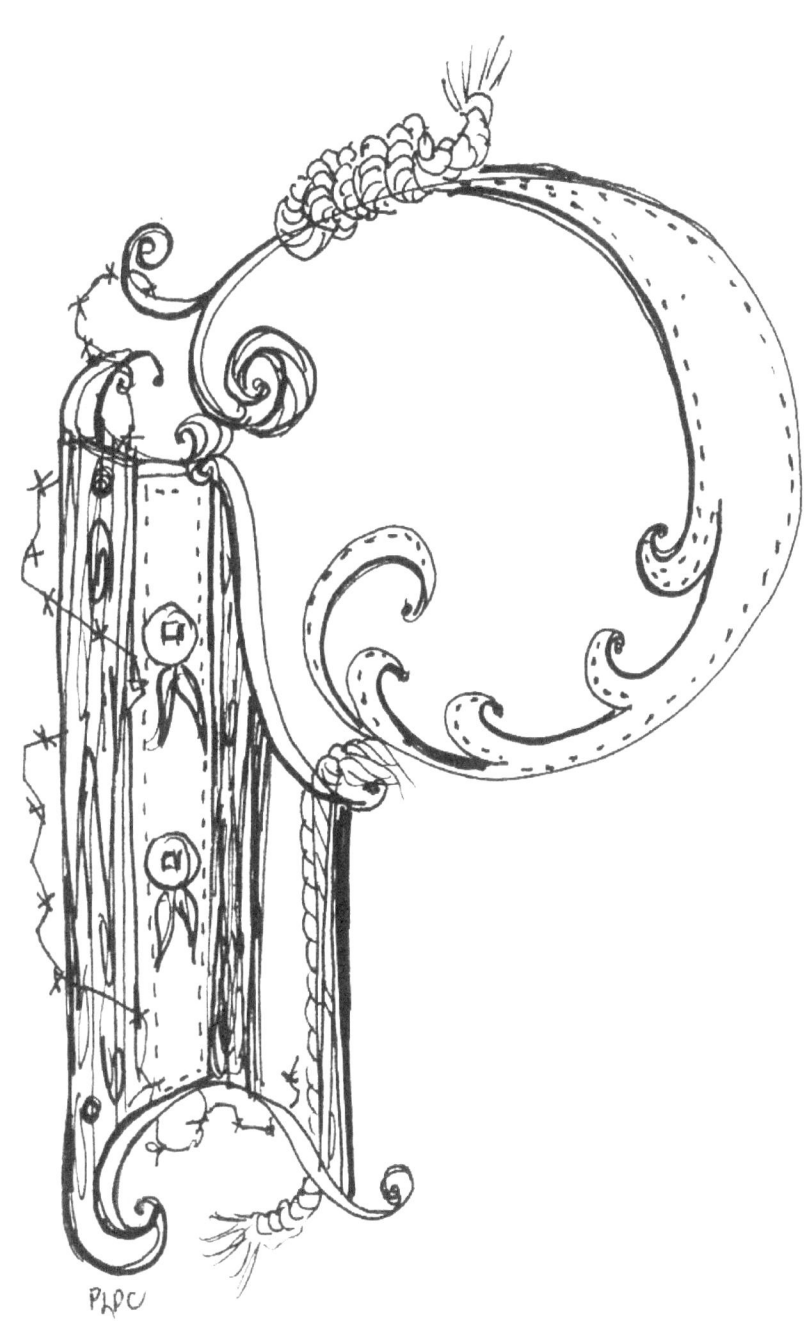

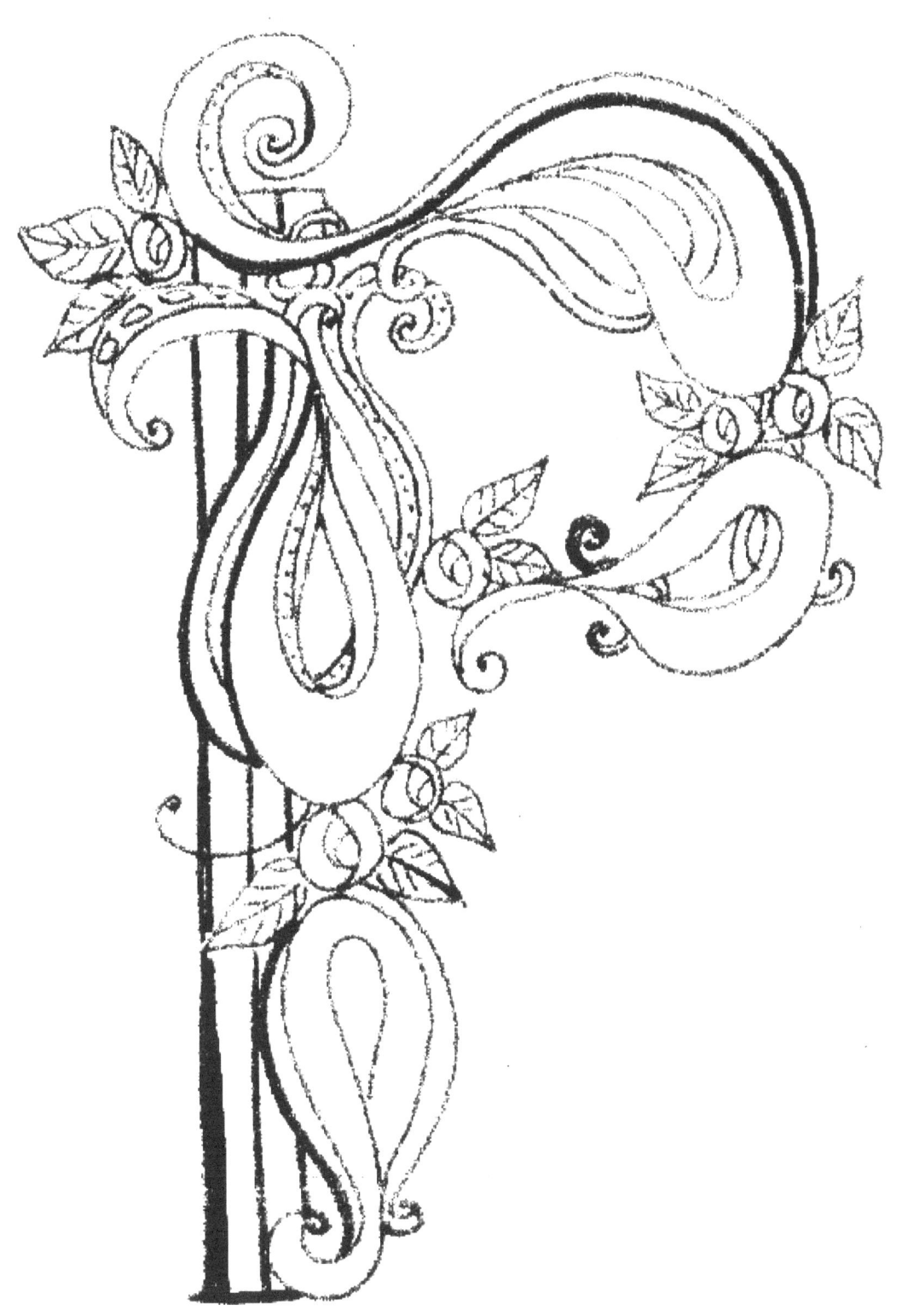

P is for pleasant, passionate, powerful, peaceful, and perfect.

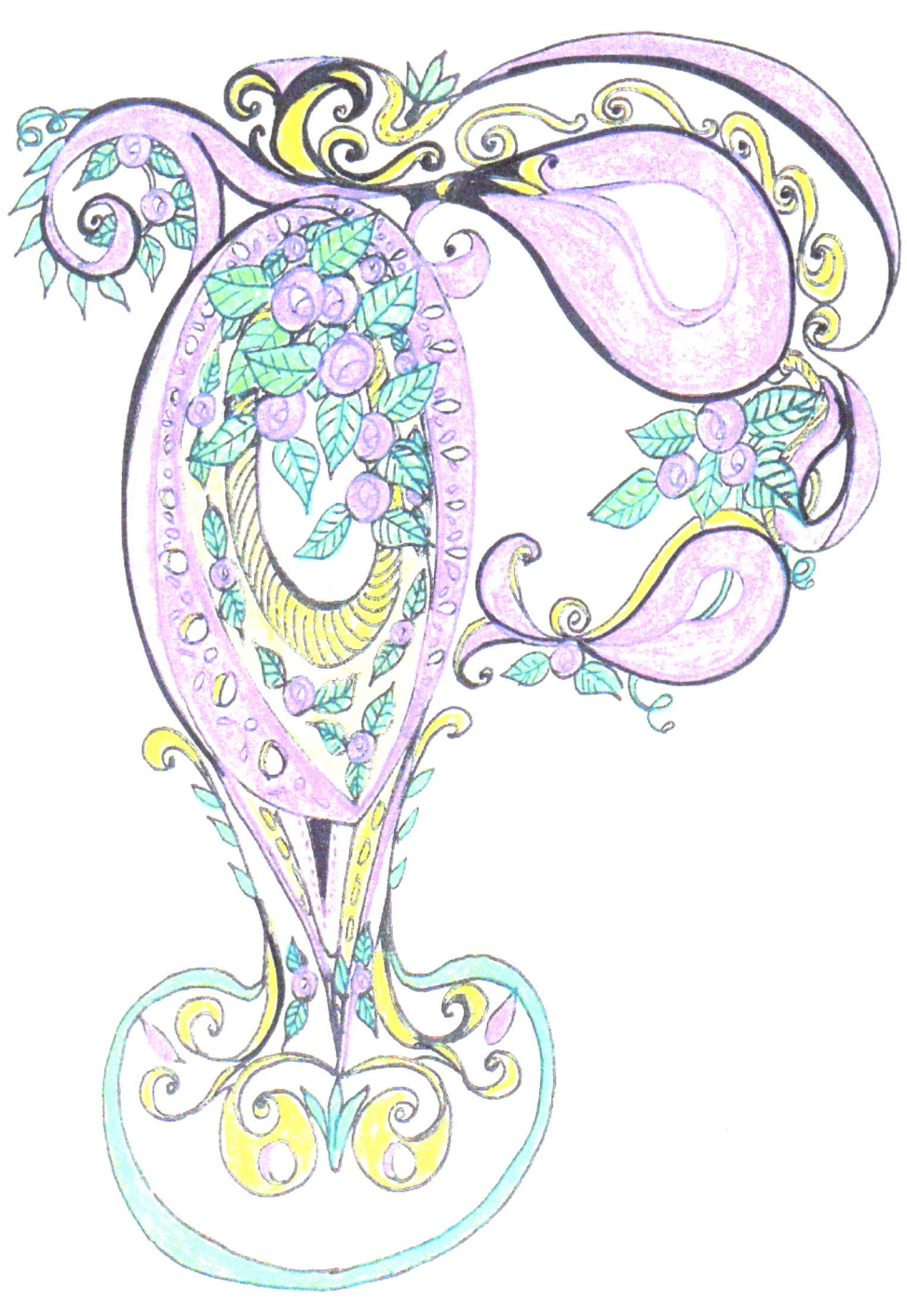

Can you find some of these letter P's in this book?

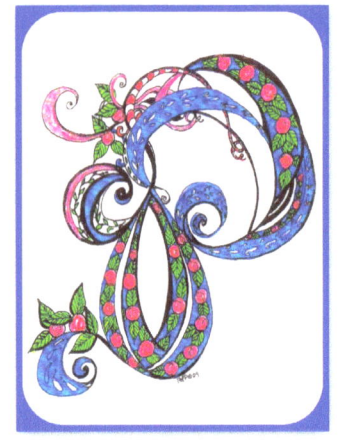 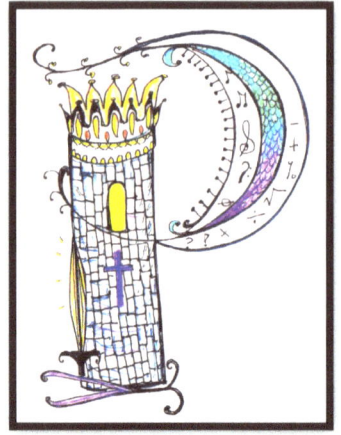 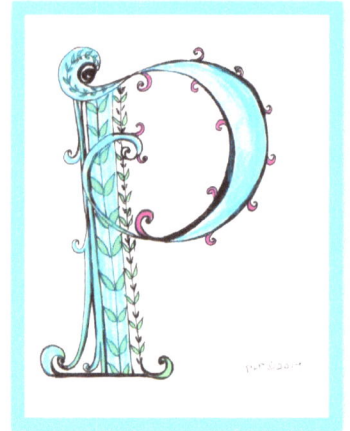

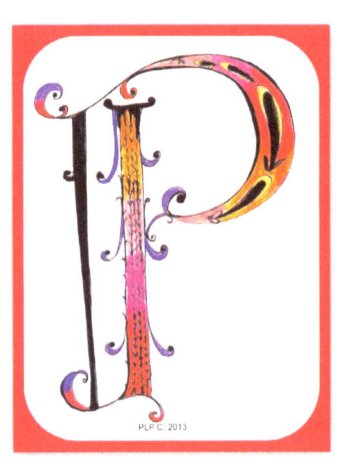 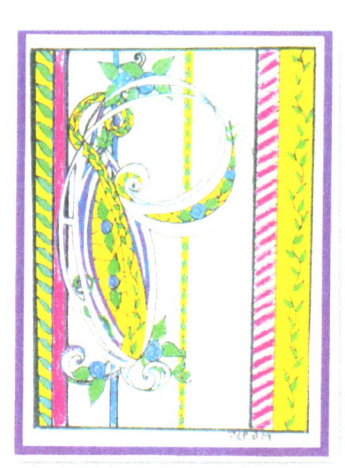 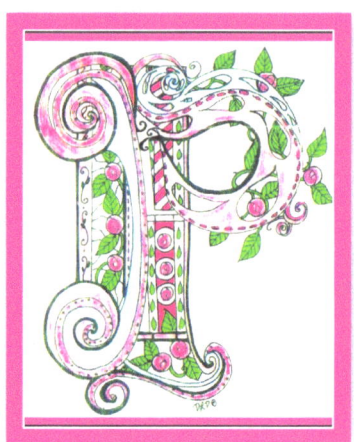

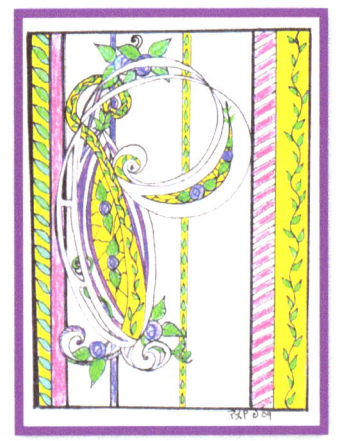 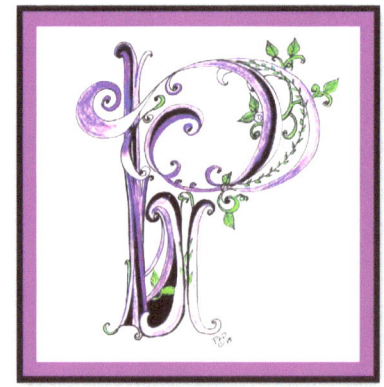 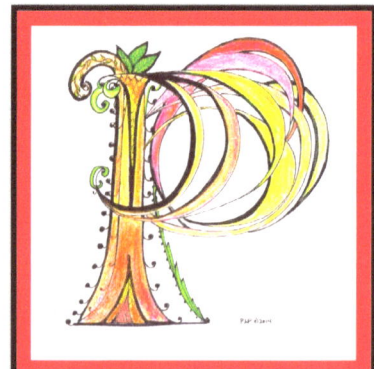

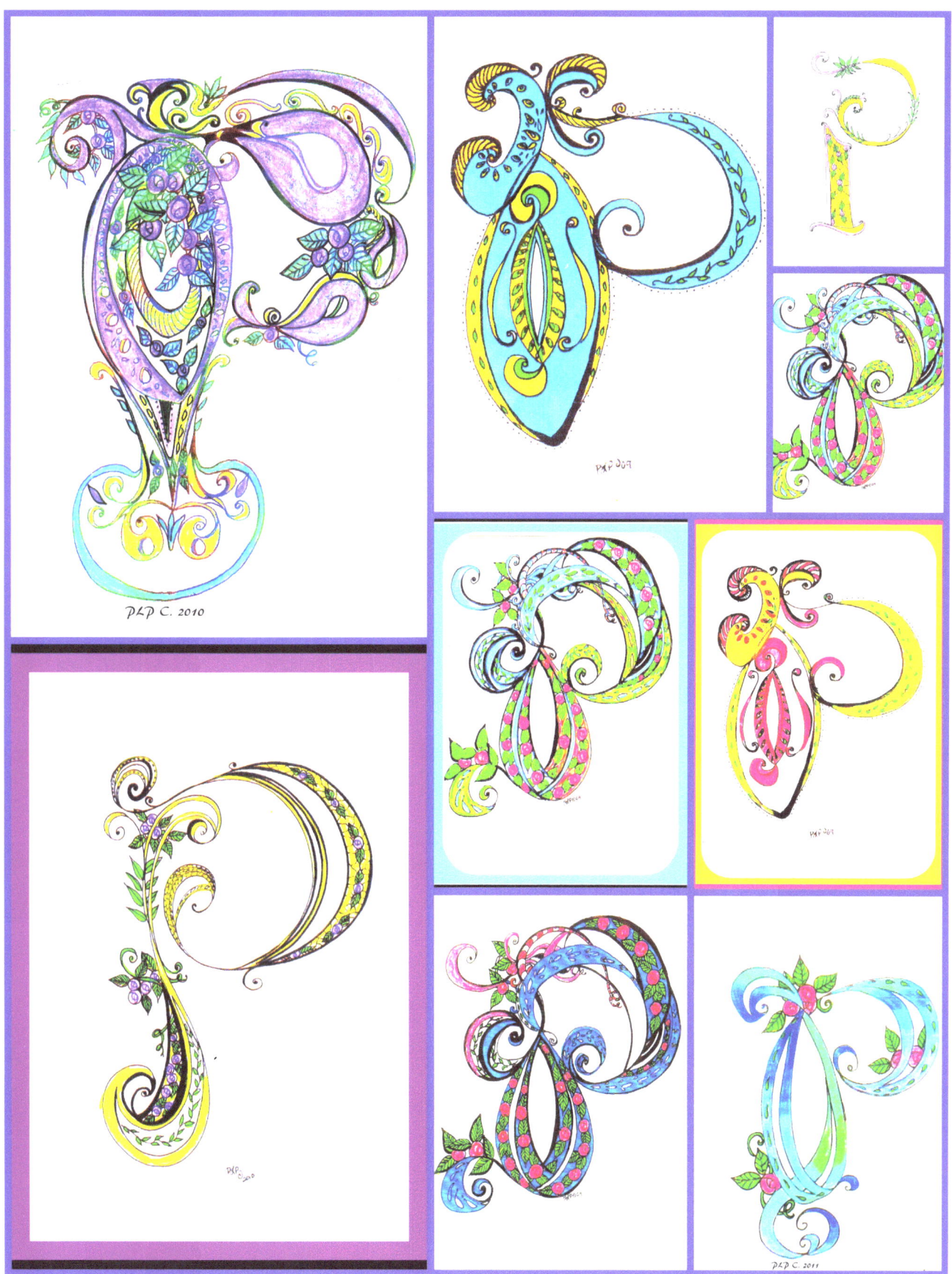

Look for more Letter Books to color
by Artist Peggy Louise Parrish.

The artist and creator of this artistic work is Peggy Parrish. She lives in Parma , Idaho. Her hobbies of drawing and coloring have led her to doodle and draw several types of artwork. Her compilation over the years is being released in the form of Adult Coloring Books with a Bandana Theme. She also enjoys drawing the faces of Children from different ethnic backgrounds and fancy lettering. This work is only a small tip of the coloring "iceberg" she has to offer. She herself likes to sit and color to relax. Her hope is that you too will enjoy coloring and find great pleasure in doing so.

Peggy Louise Parrish

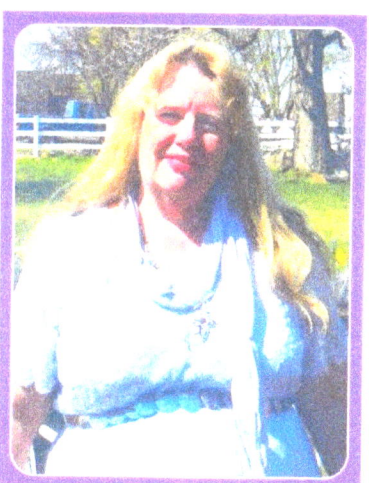

Keep watching for more Adult Coloring Books by this artist and author.

"MAY THE LORD BLESS THE WORKS OF MY HANDS AND YOURS"

www.ingramcontent.com/pod-product-compliance
Lightning Source LLC
Chambersburg PA
CBHW050750180526
45159CB00003B/1407